Your Government:
How It Works

The U.S. Secret Service

Ann Graham Gaines

Arthur M. Schlesinger, jr.
Senior Consulting Editor

Chelsea House Publishers
Philadelphia

CHELSEA HOUSE PUBLISHERS
Production Manager Pamela Loos
Art Director Sara Davis
Director of Photography Judy L. Hasday
Managing Editor James D. Gallagher
Senior Production Editor J. Christopher Higgins

Staff for THE U.S. SECRET SERVICE
Project Editor/Publishing Coordinator Jim McAvoy
Associate Art Director Takeshi Takahashi
Series Designers Takeshi Takahashi, Keith Trego
Editorial Assistant Rob Quinn

The Chelsea House World Wide Web address is
http://www.chelseahouse.com

First Printing
1 3 5 7 9 8 6 4 2

Library of Congress Cataloging-in-Publication Data

Gaines, Ann.
    The U.S. Secret Service / Ann Gaines
        p. cm. — (Your government—how it works)
    Includes bibliographical references and index.
    ISBN 0-7910-5990-1 (alk. paper)
    1. United States. Secret Service—Juvenile literature. [1. United
States. Secret Service.] I. Title: US Secret Service. II. Title.
III. Series.

HV8144.S43 G35 2000
363.28—dc21   00-047489

Contents

Government:
Crises of Confidence
  Arthur M. Schlesinger, jr.   5

1 Assassination!   9

2 The History of the
   Secret Service   17

3 Protecting the President   29

4 Money Matters   51

5 The Future   57

   Glossary   61

   Further Reading   62

   Index   63

YOUR GOVERNMENT HOW IT WORKS

The Attorney General's Office
The Cabinet
The Central Intelligence Agency
The Drug Enforcement Administration
The Federal Bureau of Investigation
The History of the Democratic Party
The History of the Republican Party
The History of Third Parties
The House of Representatives
How a Bill Is Passed
How to Become an Elected Official
The Impeachment Process
The Internal Revenue Service
The Presidency
The Secretary of State
The Senate
The Speaker of the House of Representatives
The Supreme Court
The U.S. Armed Forces
The U.S. Constitution
The U.S. Secret Service
The Vice Presidency

Introduction

Government: Crises of Confidence

Arthur M. Schlesinger, jr.

FROM THE START, Americans have regarded their government with a mixture of reliance and mistrust. The men who founded the republic understood the importance of government. "If men were angels," observed the 51st Federalist Paper, "no government would be necessary." But men are not angels. Because human beings are subject to wicked as well as to noble impulses, government was deemed essential to assure freedom and order.

The American revolutionaries, however, also knew that government could become a source of injury and oppression. The men who gathered in Philadelphia in 1787 to write the Constitution therefore had two purposes in mind: They wanted to establish a strong central authority and to limit that central authority's capacity to abuse its power.

To prevent the abuse of power, the Founding Fathers wrote two basic principles into the Constitution. The principle of federalism divided power between the state governments and the central authority. The principle of the separation of powers subdivided the central authority itself into three branches—the executive, the legislative, and the judiciary—so that "each may be a check on the other."

YOUR GOVERNMENT: HOW IT WORKS examines some of the major parts of that central authority, the federal government. It explains how various officials, agencies, and departments operate and explores the political organizations that have grown up to serve the needs of government.

Introduction

The federal government as presented in the Constitution was more an idealistic construct than a practical administrative structure. It was barely functional when it came into being.

This was especially true of the executive branch. The Constitution did not describe the executive branch in any detail. After vesting executive power in the president, it assumed the existence of "executive departments" without specifying what these departments should be. Congress began defining their functions in 1789 by creating the Departments of State, Treasury, and War.

President Washington, assisted by Secretary of the Treasury Alexander Hamilton, equipped the infant republic with a working administrative structure. Congress also continued that process by creating more executive departments as they were needed.

Throughout the 19th century, the number of federal government workers increased at a consistently faster rate than did the population. Increasing concerns about the politicization of public service led to efforts—bitterly opposed by politicians—to reform it in the latter part of the century.

The 20th century saw considerable expansion of the federal establishment. More importantly, it saw growing impatience with bureaucracy in society as a whole.

The Great Depression during the 1930s confronted the nation with its greatest crisis since the Civil War. Under Franklin Roosevelt, the New Deal reshaped the federal government, assigning it a variety of new responsibilities and greatly expanding its regulatory functions. By 1940, the number of federal workers passed the 1 million mark.

Critics complained of big government and bureaucracy. Business owners resented federal regulation. Conservatives worried about the impact of paternalistic government on self-reliance, on community responsibility, and on economic and personal freedom.

When the United States entered World War II in 1941, government agencies focused their energies on supporting the war effort. By the end of World War II, federal civilian employment had risen to 3.8 million. With peace, the federal establishment declined to around 2 million in 1950. Then growth resumed, reaching 2.8 million by the 1980s.

A large part of this growth was the result of the national government assuming new functions such as: affirmative action in civil rights, environmental protection, and safety and health in the workplace.

Some critics became convinced that the national government was a steadily growing behemoth swallowing up the liberties of the people. The 1980s brought new intensity to the debate about government growth. Foes of Washington bureaucrats preferred local government, feeling it more responsive to popular needs.

But local government is characteristically the government of the locally powerful. Historically, the locally powerless have often won their human and constitutional rights by appealing to the national government. The national government has defended racial justice against local bigotry, upheld the Bill of Rights against local vigilantism, and protected natural resources from local greed. It has civilized industry and secured the rights of labor organizations. Had the states' rights creed prevailed, perhaps slavery would still exist in the United States.

Americans are still of two minds. When pollsters ask large, spacious questions—Do you think government has become too involved in your lives? Do you think government should stop regulating business?—a sizable majority opposes big government. But when asked specific questions about the practical work of government—Do you favor Social Security? Unemployment compensation? Medicare? Health and safety standards in factories? Environmental protection?—a sizable majority approves of intervention.

We do not like bureaucracy, but we cannot live without it. We need its genius for organizing the intricate details of our daily lives. Without bureaucracy, modern society would collapse. It would be impossible to run any of the large public and private organizations we depend on without bureaucracy's division of labor and hierarchy of authority. The challenge is to keep these necessary structures of our civilization flexible, efficient, and capable of innovation.

More than 200 years after the drafting of the Constitution, Americans still rely on government but also mistrust it. These attitudes continue to serve us well. What we mistrust, we are more likely to monitor. And government needs our constant attention if it is to avoid inefficiency, incompetence, and arbitrariness. Without our informed participation, it cannot serve us individually or help us as a people to attain the lofty goals of the Founding Fathers.

President McKinley's assassination may not have occurred if the role of the Secret Service in 1901 was similar to that of today's agency. In more recent years, the protection of the president of the United States has become the organization's primary role.

CHAPTER 1

Assassination!

PRESIDENT WILLIAM MCKINLEY was a very friendly man whom most Americans liked. After a morning in his White House office, McKinley enjoyed going out for a walk around downtown Washington, D.C. Passers-by often stopped him to thank him for bringing the country out of an economic **depression** and winning the Spanish-American War. McKinley shook their hands with a big smile on his face.

In 1901, McKinley began his second term as president. He had been reelected in a **landslide**. It was a very happy time for many Americans. They had food on their tables, money in their pockets, and a sense of hope.

Immigrants flocked to the United States from Europe. Here their lives would be hard. Most lived in crowded **tenements.** Even their children had to work long hours, often in factories filled with dangerous

President William McKinley was shot on September 6, 1901, and later died from his wounds. Today, people may find it surprising that he was escorted by only one Secret Service agent at the time of the attack.

T. DART WALKER
BUFFALO

machinery. Still, they regarded America as the land of opportunity.

To celebrate its progress, the United States held several world's fairs. The Pan-American Exposition was held in Buffalo, New York. Thousands of visitors strolled through its buildings filled with displays of inventions and other wonders.

Newspapers announced that President McKinley would be at a reception hall at the Pan-American Exposition on September 6, 1901. A crowd turned out, eager to meet him. He arrived in the company of 11 soldiers and a Secret Service agent. He and the other honored guests formed a line: anybody who wished to could approach to meet them. McKinley chatted and joked with his well-wishers.

The room filled with cheerful noise. McKinley bent over to give a child the carnation from his buttonhole. Straightening up, he saw a man coming toward him. A white cloth covered his right hand. Everybody thought it was a bandage. But the cloth really covered a revolver. Pushing aside the hand the president held out, the **assassin** placed his gun right on McKinley's chest. He pulled the trigger twice. The shots sounded like cracks of a whip.

Silence fell. McKinley stared at the stranger, then toppled to the ground. Blood poured from his wounds. People rushed to help him. He begged them not to tell his sick wife that he had been shot. Soldiers jumped on the assassin and forced him to the floor. They started to beat him. He covered his head and whimpered. McKinley called out, "Be easy with him, boys."

In jail, the shooter told the police his name was Leon Czolgosz (pronounced Chol'-gosh). Because of his name, people believed he was a foreigner. This was not true: he had been born in the United States. He was an **anarchist.** At the time, many Europeans were becoming unhappy with their governments. They wanted reforms. Anarchists were reformers who believed that governments should not exist. People could rule themselves, they said. Czolgosz was one of the few anarchists who then lived in the United States. He hoped shooting President McKinley would make the government collapse.

At first, it seemed like McKinley would recover. Surgeons removed one bullet from his body. His vice president, Theodore Roosevelt, was so sure that everything would be all right that he went on vacation. He hiked high up in the Adirondack Mountains. But while Roosevelt was camping, McKinley suddenly got much worse.

Leon Czolgosz was given the death penalty for the assassination of President McKinley. Czolgosz was an anarchist who believed that all forms of government were wrong and should be removed by any means necessary.

He fell into a coma. A guide was sent into the Adirondacks to track down Roosevelt and deliver the message that he must hurry back to Washington, D.C. To get down from the mountains, Roosevelt traveled all night in a wagon.

On the morning of September 14, 1901, Roosevelt arrived at the railroad station where he planned to board a train for Washington. There he found out that William McKinley had just died. His death did not result in disorder, as Czolgosz had hoped. Within hours, Roosevelt was sworn in as president. Congress and other branches of the government kept working. A funeral train carried McKinley's body back to his home town in Ohio. People lined the railroad tracks to watch his casket go by.

Czolgosz was charged with murder. His trial started and ended quickly. The judge sentenced him to death. Just a few weeks later, Czolgosz died in the electric chair.

Today it amazes many Americans to learn that President McKinley went for walks by himself. They are also surprised that he went to a big public event with just one Secret Service agent. But back then the president had no full-time bodyguards.

The Secret Service was a very different **agency** than it is today. Since it was founded in 1865, the agency's number one job had been to stop **counterfeiting**. Congress gave it other responsibilities, too, but they were less important. Protecting the president was just one of many things Secret Service agents did.

Today, Americans think more about danger than they did a hundred years ago. They know many **terrorists** would like to kill the president. Today, the Secret Service's biggest job is protection of the president.

And the president is not the only person the agency protects. Congress has also ordered it to keep safe the president's family, the vice president and his family, presidential candidates, former presidents, and foreign leaders who come to the United States.

But the Secret Service has many other duties, too. The agency still fulfills its original mission. It investigates forgery (illegal manufacture) of American coins, currency, stamps, or government bonds. New laws have put the agency in charge of **investigating** fake checks and credit cards. Agents investigate cases of identity theft (in which one person starts using another's

The wreckage of a small plane lies next to the White House on September 12, 1994. The pilot was killed in the crash after having breached the White House's restricted airspace. The president faces threats from all sides, and it is the goal of the Secret Service to ensure his safety.

name and personal information). Also, they hunt down people who break (or hack) into the government's computer systems.

In order to fulfill all of these responsibilities, the Secret Service employs 5,000 people who work in offices scattered all over the United States and around the globe. The job requires intelligence and dedication. Sometimes Secret Service agents have to display courage, too. Those who protect the president, especially, often risk their lives. Agents have died on duty. Bodyguards have to be ready at any moment to throw themselves in the line of fire, to use their bodies to shield the person they protect. Its duties make the Secret Service one of the most important of all

federal agencies. Given the fact that we live during an age
of terrorist threats and high-tech crime, the U.S. Secret
Service will most likely become even more important in
the future.

CHAPTER 2

The History of the Secret Service

A SPY HIDES IN THE woods along a road. He peers out and watches an enemy army march by. He counts how many soldiers are on the move and notices what kinds of weapons they carry.

The spy works for a general who will want to know, too, about the enemy's spirits. How do the soldiers act? Are they afraid, jumping at sudden noises? Or do they look confident? If they sing and joke, they probably expect to win their next battle. Sometimes a spy simply memorizes the facts he gathers. Other times he or she writes them down in code. As soon as possible, he will send a message or sneak back to his own army to report.

Army leaders have depended on spies for thousands of years. In 500 B.C., a Chinese book called *The Art of War* told all about spies. They have played a part in American history, too. During the American Revolution, George Washington sent many spies out to gather information for him.

Although President Abraham Lincoln used the services of bodyguards during the Civil War, he did not continue that habit following the war's end. An angered Southerner by the name of John Wilkes Booth took advantage of Lincoln's lack of an armed escort and shot the president on April 14, 1865. He died the following day.

Nathan Hale was one of them. In 1776, Hale was in New York. The British army had taken over the city. Hale pretended to be an art teacher loyal to the king. He was within close proximity to the army all the time. Redcoats (British soldiers) started to suspect him of spying. When they looked in his sketchbooks they found no drawings of scenery. Instead, he had been recording how big the enemy's cannons were and what kind of fortifications they had built. He planned to pass on to Washington everything he knew. Today, Americans remember Hale because just before the British hanged him, he is said to have uttered these stirring words: "I only regret that I have but one life to lose for my country."

During the Civil War, both the North and South used spies. Their armies called their spies as a group the "bureau of secret service." The Union army's secret service was founded when a detective named Allan Pinkerton found out that a group of Southerners had hatched a plot to **assassinate** Abraham Lincoln. The Union army asked Pinkerton to hire a group of men to protect the president. They also did some spying. According to one historian, "[Pinkerton] . . . established America's first federal intelligence agency."

The army's secret service shut down soon after the war. But on July 5, 1865, the U.S. federal government established a new agency called the Secret Service. It was part of the Treasury Department, not the army. The new Secret Service had just one job—to prevent counterfeiting.

During the Civil War, Americans used many kinds of money. The federal government did not print money or make coins, states did. Banks issued their own money, too. At one point, there were 1,600 different kinds of banknotes in use.

In 1862, the U.S. Treasury started to issue "greenbacks." But the old kinds of money were still used after the war, too. Counterfeiting became a big problem: according to the Secret Service, "one-third to one-half of the currency in circulation . . . was counterfeit." It was hard to tell fake and real money apart. Only experts could tell for sure whether money was real.

Fake money caused trouble for Americans. There were not many jobs in the South right after the war. Prices rose very high everywhere. Most people needed every cent they had for necessities like bread and coal. So it was a problem when a shopkeeper told them he thought their money was fake and refused to take it.

Earlier, local policemen and sheriffs had been in charge of arresting counterfeiters. But in 1863, the federal government's Treasury Department started to hunt down counterfeiters. The Treasury Department sent employees across the nation. They acted like detectives, following clues to find out where fake bills came from. They made many arrests, which pleased Congress. It was decided by Congress that stopping counterfeiting should become the permanent responsibility of the Treasury Department. As part of the department, it created the Secret Service agency. William

A Secret Service agent examines a sheet of counterfeit bills. The original goal of the Secret Service was to apprehend counterfeiters, and, although its responsibilities have grown, that mission has remained the same.

P. Wood was its first chief. The agency's headquarters were located in Washington, D.C.

Soon the Secret Service had 30 employees, called agents. Some of them had been spies during the Civil War. Others had experience as detectives. Still others had been criminals. Wood hired criminals because he believed their experience would make them good at spotting other crooks.

But hiring criminals did not work out well. In the first Secret Service handbook, published in 1868, the chief had to include rules against drinking alcohol on the job and accepting bribes. The next year, Hiram C. Whitley became the agency's new chief. He made some big changes. He replaced the former criminals with businessmen. He moved Secret Service headquarters to New York City. Later the service opened offices in many cities and its headquarters moved back to Washington.

The goal of the Secret Service was to stop counterfeit money from being made. Secret Service agents removed counterfeit money they found from circulation. But what they really wanted was to send counterfeiters to jail.

To counterfeit paper money took special skills. The best counterfeiters examined real money a quarter-inch at a time. Then they copied a bill, including every last detail, even tiny dots. Once they had engraved a copy backward onto an **engraving** plate, they bought exactly the same kind of paper and ink the Treasury used for its money. Then they printed their bills.

Sometimes counterfeiters worked in secret workshops. Some owned print shops. By day they printed books. But at night they made money. Some people used a tiny press to print bills out one at a time on their kitchen table. They hung them up to dry over the bathtub.

Secret Service agents use many methods to find counterfeiters. Sometimes agents disguised themselves and went undercover. They made up new names for themselves and moved into neighborhoods where counterfeiters were suspected to be working. Sometimes agents pretended they wanted to buy fake money. Counterfeiters sold other crooks fake money. This way lessened the chance they would be caught. The agents arrested counterfeiters who offered to sell them phony money.

Sometimes agents pretended to be counterfeiters. After all, they knew a great deal about the business. They went to work for a real counterfeiter. As soon as he started work on a fake bill, they arrested him.

Some agents shadowed suspects, hoping to catch them buying supplies for counterfeiting. Others looked through suspects' mail. They wanted to find letters proving they were guilty. In the early days, agents used a lot of informers. They would get one counterfeiter to tell them about others.

In the early 20th century, an agent named Don Wilkie remembered how one counterfeiter worked. "The Sausage Man" worked by himself. He made just a few fake $10 bills at a time. To get rid of them, he would go to a grocery store and buy ten cents worth of sausage. This meant he got $9.90 back in real money.

The Sausage Man kept this up for a long time. He moved from place to place. He would use just 10 or 12 bills in a row and then lay low, letting his trail grow cold. He liked to go to banks and look at posters they put up warning people about counterfeit bills. To help people figure out which bills were fake, they always described in detail errors counterfeiters had made. He would look for a poster that described a bill he had made. He found out what his mistakes were. Then he went back and fixed the plate he used to make his money! Thus, his counterfeiting got better and better.

After searching for the Sausage Man for years, Secret Service agents finally arrested him without trouble. But many other times, agents faced terrible danger when making arrests. Some counterfeiters carried weapons. It did not bother them to kill people who got in their way. Hoping to inflict extra pain on any Secret Service agent who got too close, one counterfeiter loaded his gun not just with bullets and gunpowder, but with nails, steel scrapings, and bolts, too. Agents were very lucky the gun sat just out of his reach when they burst into his hideout. Another counterfeiter was a world-class knife-thrower. He picked up a deadly dagger when agents approached him. Luckily, they had their guns ready. An agent shot him in the wrist just before he threw his weapon.

In 1897, the Secret Service broke up one of the biggest counterfeiting conspiracies of all time. A bank sent the Treasury Department a suspicious bill. At first Treasury Department officials thought it was real. But they took a look at it under a microscope. It was seen to have one tiny flaw. The top of one letter *s* looked funny. Agents enlarged photographs of the bill. This showed them that the plate used to print the bills had been engraved by both a man and a machine.

They realized one man could not have produced the plate by himself. Agents knew a photoengraver had teamed up with someone who engraved by hand. It took months for the Secret Service to find a photoengraver and a regular engraver who owned a shop together. They had recently started to spend a lot of money, and spying revealed their secret workshop.

Agents needed to get a copy of their key and get into their hideout. They pretended to open a theater in the neighborhood. They met a boy who ran errands for the suspects. They asked him to audition for a play. While he was onstage in costume, an agent went through the pockets of the boy's clothes, found his keys, and copied them.

All this effort paid off. The Secret Service got the evidence they needed. They found out their suspects belonged to a gang of counterfeiters who had planned to get fake bills worth $10 million into circulation. Two of them had been leading double lives: they worked for the government.

Between 1865 and 1900, Secret Service agents arrested more than 100,000 counterfeiters. But they performed other tasks, too. In 1867, just two years after establishing the agency, Congress placed the Secret Service in charge of "detecting persons perpetrating frauds against the government." This meant agents got called in whenever someone was accused of cheating the government. Agents investigated illegal voting and mail robbery. They used their skills to find out what had happened to money missing from government funds. They also arrested smugglers, criminals who brought illegal goods into the country.

One of the Secret Service's biggest concerns during the late 19th and early 20th centuries was land **fraud.** The federal government owned huge pieces of land out West. It gave homesteads to anyone who agreed to farm land. Thousands of families went West in covered wagons to claim land. But many crooks also cheated the government in order to get land. Some land titles went to people who had never set foot outside of New York City. Secret Service agents investigated many cases of land fraud. In one case, an agent discovered that the governor of Oklahoma, among other people, had cheated Native Americans out of land worth millions of dollars.

In 1907, Secret Service operative Joseph A. Walker was murdered in cold blood while investigating another case of fraud out West. In Colorado, a large coal company was suspected of having dug tunnels under government land. Agents thought the people who ran the company were using the tunnels to mine coal from government land. Four agents set out to look for the tunnels. Coming upon an air shaft that led down into one of the tunnels, they laid a railroad tie, a long, thick beam, across the hole. They looped a rope around the tie and slid down it to the bottom of the air shaft. Then they set out to explore the tunnel they had found. Walker stayed up top because he suffered from asthma and could not breathe underground.

The coal company officials had realized they were being investigated. They did not want to be arrested. So they hired killers to assassinate the Secret Service agents. When the agents set out from town, the hired guns followed them. They sneaked up on Walker and shot him in the back. Instead of going down into the tunnel to kill the other Secret Service agents, too, they just cut the rope the agents had used to go down into the tunnels. They thought the agents would get stuck underground and die of starvation down there. But this did not happen. After they had proved the tunnels led to the coal company, the other agents came back to the air shaft. Using their hands and feet, they made an extremely dangerous climb up.

Another crime the Secret Service investigated was illegal immigration. The law said exactly how many people could come to the United States from different countries. Businessmen in Chinatown in San Francisco, California, were sneaking other people into the country from China. They told the people they smuggled in that they would give them good jobs here. But they really planned to essentially make them slaves. They would make the women work as prostitutes.

In 1907, the Secret Service launched an investigation into the smuggling of Chinese immigrants. Working undercover, agent Don Wilkie pretended to be a bum. He let his beard grow long and scruffy. He started to sleep in his suit, which he wore every single day. He moved to Chinatown, where he applied for two jobs. The first was in a grocery store. He stocked its displays with Chinese vegetables and dried ducks. The second was in an opium den, a place where people went to smoke the illegal narcotic.

Gradually Wilkie became taken for granted by the people of the neighborhood. They never questioned what he was doing. They failed to figure out that in his spare time he shadowed suspects, the people he thought were smuggling in the Chinese immigrants. Finally, he actually witnessed Chinese immigrants being smuggled off a boat and onto a wharf and arrested the plot's masterminds. Next he

Members of the Ku Klux Klan gather around a burning cross. The Secret Service has often been asked to take on special assignments, including infiltrating groups such as the KKK.

got assigned to Laredo, Texas. The government had gotten another tip: Chinese people were being brought into the country illegally on trains from Mexico. One night he found seven Chinese people in a train's water tank. Three had drowned.

The Secret Service was also asked to take on special assignments. In the Spanish-American War, it tracked down enemy spies for the American government. When racists began to form the Ku Klux Klan, Secret Service agents went undercover in this group of white people who terrorized blacks. They also hunted down moonshiners, who made their own whiskey. And the Secret Service investigated the beef industry. A group of rich men who owned slaughterhouses had secretly agreed they would all charge low prices for a time in order to force their competitors out of business.

In 1898, the Secret Service still had just 35 agents and an annual budget of $100,000. But the agency grew slowly but surely throughout the 20th century. For a long time, it was the only federal government agency that undertook investigations. But this changed in 1908. That year, eight Secret Service agents transferred from the Department of the Treasury to the Department of Justice to start investigating for that office. Eventually, this led to the establishment of the Federal Bureau of Investigation, or the FBI.

Since the Secret Service was founded, its responsibilities have changed, and the agency has had many different chiefs. But one thing has stayed the same: the Secret Service has always remained part of the Treasury Department. The Secret Service chief reports to the secretary of the Treasury, no matter what type of crime his agents have been investigating.

President Ronald Reagan was shot in 1981 only a few short feet from the safety of his waiting car. Even though the Secret Service takes extreme measures to protect the president, threats are ever present and require agents to be ever vigilant.

CHAPTER **3**

Protecting the President

IN 1981, RONALD REAGAN had just begun his first term as president. On one occasion in March of that year he went to a meeting at a hotel in Washington, D.C. The Secret Service made all the usual precautions. Reagan traveled there in a car with bulletproof windows. Agents had checked out the rooms where he would be to make sure there were no bombs hidden in them. They had gone over lists provided to them of who else would attend the meeting.

Despite all this preparation, tragedy occurred. Reagan had just left the building to go back to the White House. He only had to walk a few feet to get in his car. A small crowd had gathered to see him. Secret Service agents were watching everyone. Everything seemed normal. That is, until Reagan was shot from just a few feet away by a crazed gunman. A bullet entered his lung. Later, doctors removed it without complications. His press secretary, James Brady, was not as lucky. He was also shot and would never recover entirely from his wounds.

The Secret Service did not start to protect the president full-time until 1901. Today protecting the president remains its biggest job. None of the country's early presidents ever thought they needed protection. When George Washington became president in 1789, he did not have the freedom he would have liked. He found it hard to take a walk or ride his horse through the streets of New York, one of the nation's first capitals. But this was not because his life was in danger. He was such a popular man that people crowded around whenever he went out in public. To give him more of a chance to meet and talk with the public, he and his wife, Martha, threw many parties. Thomas Jefferson felt so secure that on his inauguration day in 1801 he walked from the house where he had been staying to the Capitol building to take his oath of office. Not a single guard went with him. The city of Washington was then so new it didn't even have a police force.

Although nobody worried about the safety of the early presidents, they did sometimes face danger. When the War of 1812 broke out between the United States and Great Britain, the British army invaded the United States. Its generals wanted to capture President James Madison. British soldiers got within a few miles of him, but he always got away. Had he seemed in great danger, American soldiers would have protected him. The thought of him needing specially-trained bodyguards never occurred to anyone at the time.

Once President John Quincy Adams was threatened in the White House by an angry soldier. The soldier had been accused of a crime he said he did not commit. He shouted and waved a gun about, but Adams was not injured. In general, he never feared for his life. He even

went swimming by himself in the Potomac River. Over-all, the first six presidents were able to lead pretty ordinary lives.

The first assassination attempt on a president occurred during the second term of the seventh president. Andrew Jackson became president in 1829. On January 30, 1835, Jackson went to the Capitol. A congressman had died, and his funeral was being held there. When pallbearers picked up the casket, a procession of mourners slowly began to move out the door and down the steps toward a nearby cemetery. Jackson stopped for a minute on the portico, the walkway that runs around the Capitol building. Suddenly, a man leapt from deep shadows right out in front of him. Armed with two pistols, Richard Lawrence raised one and aimed. But when he pulled the trigger, the gun misfired.

Richard Lawrence points a pistol at President Andrew Jackson (the taller man between the two columns). The assassination attempt failed when the guns misfired. But even after the attempt on his life, Jackson continued to travel without bodyguards.

There was a little cloud of smoke but no bullet. Jackson became furious. Instead of trying to escape, he ran right at Lawrence and raised his cane to hit him.

When Jackson got right up to him, Lawrence raised his second gun. He placed it right on Jackson's chest and squeezed the trigger. But this pistol misfired, too. Jackson walked away unharmed. Davy Crockett was one of the congressmen who captured Lawrence. Lawrence proved he was insane while waiting in jail for his trial. He thought that he was supposed to be king of England but that Jackson had somehow prevented him from getting the attention he deserved. At the end of his trial he was found guilty. He spent the rest of his life in an insane asylum. Jackson thought no one else would want to kill him. He did not start using a bodyguard but kept going about as he pleased.

In August 1842, a drunk threw rocks at the 10th president, John Tyler, while he walked on the White House grounds. Congress then passed a law establishing a new watch by a captain and 15 men from the metropolitan police of Washington, D.C. Their job, however, was to guard the nation's buildings, not the president.

Abraham Lincoln was president during the most troubled time in American history. Soldiers protected him even at his inauguration (when he was sworn into office). At that point, the Civil War had not yet begun. But everybody knew fighting would soon break out between the North and South. Throughout his presidency, Lincoln received many death threats. Many bands of Southerners plotted to kidnap or kill him.

Bodyguards continued to protect Lincoln throughout the war. Sometimes soldiers did the job, just as at his inauguration. But other times it was policemen. Lincoln hated being constantly watched. Sometimes he wanted time alone so badly that he slipped away from his guards. But other times he worried that his life was at risk. He knew that if he were to die it would be harder for the Union to win the war. So when threats seemed especially bad, he hired a private bodyguard.

By April 1865, the Civil War was coming to a close. On April 5, Confederate General Robert E. Lee and most of the Confederate army surrendered to Union General Ulysses S. Grant at Appomattox, Virginia. Confederate General Joseph Johnston and some of his soldiers kept fighting. But Union General William Sherman was expected soon to force him and his men to lay down their arms, too. Everybody knew that the South had lost the war.

On April 14, the mood in Washington, D.C., was happy. Having worked virtually nonstop for years, the president decided he could take some time to enjoy himself. He went for a carriage ride with his wife in the afternoon. That night, they planned to go see a play at Ford's Theater. Lots of people knew this. The newspaper announced that they had reserved special seats.

The president, his wife, and two friends, Miss Clara Harris and Major Henry Rathbone, arrived at the theater late, after the curtain had already gone up. They entered the presidential box, which had the best seats in the house. Four chairs sat on a fancy balcony that was just above the stage. When the actors realized the president had arrived in his box, they stopped the play. The theater's orchestra struck up "Hail to the Chief." The audience cheered, and Lincoln came forward to bow and wave. When he sat down, the actors went on with the play.

John F. Parker was the policeman who had been assigned to protect Lincoln that night. Lincoln was receiving fewer threats to his life, but the government knew he was still in some danger because Southerners felt so angry about having been defeated in the war.

John Wilkes Booth aims his pistol at the head of President Abraham Lincoln during a performance at Ford's Theater in Washington, D.C. Lincoln employed a team of bodyguards during the Civil War, but, following the war's end, returned to his habit of traveling unprotected.

Parker stayed outside in the corridor for a while. But then he left his post. Lincoln's carriage driver, who had been parked outside the theater, later said he and Parker had gone for a drink in a nearby saloon.

A Confederate named John Wilkes Booth came into the building when the play was about halfway through. Booth made his living as an actor. Before the war, he had appeared in many plays at this theater. So he knew his way around Ford's. He sneaked into the corridor that led to the presidential box. Finding no guard there, he turned around and jammed the door to the corridor shut.

Silently, he opened the door between the corridor and the box where Lincoln sat. The play was a comedy. The actors were clowning around onstage, and Lincoln and the rest of the audience laughed heartily. Booth quickly walked from the door to right behind Lincoln's chair. No one noticed him. Lifting a revolver, Booth shot Lincoln in the back of the head.

The sound of the shot made Major Rathbone leap right out of his own chair. He tried to grab Booth, who dropped his gun and pulled out a knife. Booth slashed at Rathbone, cutting his arm. The audience began to realize that something terrible had happened. As they watched, Booth got away from Rathbone. He jumped right out of the presidential box. As he went over the edge, his spur caught on a curtain. Booth dangled over the stage and then fell heavily. The fall broke his left leg, but Booth picked himself up. Hobbling, he ran across the stage to an exit at the back. He flung open the door. Out in the street, Booth clambered onto the horse he had tied there and rode off into the night.

Back in the theater, the audience was in an uproar. People shouted and pointed. Mary Lincoln was screaming. Doctors who had come to watch the play rushed to Lincoln's side. They lay him down and examined the huge wound in the back of his head. But they could do nothing more. There was no way he could recover from his wound. They carried him to a nearby house. Abraham Lincoln died the next morning. It was one of the saddest times in all of American history.

Booth hid out for 12 days. But Union soldiers finally tracked him down. He had escaped far out into the country where he was hiding in a barn. When the soldiers rode up, he refused to come out. To make him, soldiers set it on fire. Sure this would bring him out, they placed their rifles on their shoulders. When he appeared in the doorway, he was shot and killed.

A Congressional committee investigated the assassination. Its members found out Booth had been plotting the assassination for a very long time. In fact, he was part of a group of conspirators that had planned to kill not just

Lincoln but also his vice president and other government officials. The committee wrote a report that explained in great detail what happened. But it never said a word about a need for presidents to be protected. One explanation for this may be that at the time Americans saw Lincoln's assassination "as part of a unique crisis."

In the years that followed, presidents traveled without bodyguards. A few metropolitan policemen patrolled the White House grounds. But their job was to make sure that no one broke in and stole valuables. No one saw a need for them to protect the very important man who lived there. Servants let people in and out to meet the president.

Again this lack of protection led to tragedy. James Garfield became president in 1881. A businessman named Charles J. Guiteau had begun to have mental problems. He had been one of many people who campaigned for Garfield when he was running for president. The Republican Party had not asked him to do so. Garfield did not know him. But Guiteau believed that it was due to his own efforts that Garfield had been elected. Guiteau felt Garfield owed him a political job. He wrote to him many times to request he be appointed a diplomat. Garfield never answered.

Upset, Guiteau started to stalk the president. On July 2, 1881, Guiteau came up behind Garfield in a train station and shot him in the back. Garfield lived for two months but finally died from his wound on September 19, 1881. At his trial, Guiteau said God ordered him to kill the president. Guiteau was hanged for his crime on June 30, 1882.

After Garfield died, an article in the *New York Times* predicted that in the future the president would be "the slave of his office." By saying this, the author of the article meant that the risk of being assassinated would mean the president could not do anything by himself. He would not be allowed to go anywhere except with guards who would tell him where and when he could safely go places. He would be "the prisoner of . . . restrictions." But that did not happen. Congress did not insist that the president use bodyguards. Presidents continued to see no need for them.

Finally, toward the end of the 19th century, government officials began to worry about the safety of the president. During his second term President Grover Cleveland received many threats on his life. His wife became so upset, he agreed to hire more policemen to patrol the White House grounds. But he never gave in to her and used a bodyguard.

Nevertheless, after 1894, Secret Service agents began to protect him without his knowing it. While investigating something else, they had found that a group of gamblers planned to kill Cleveland. They were determined to prevent that from happening. When he left Washington on vacation, agents followed. They hid around his summer house to watch him with binoculars. He did not know they were there until they told him. From that point on, he let Secret Service agents go along with him when he was going somewhere they thought might be dangerous. But he never liked it.

During the Spanish-American War, the government thought President William McKinley needed protection. Officials worried that the enemy might send spies to kill him. Congress ordered Secret Service guards to protect him even when he was at home in the White House. After the war ended, this stopped. But then there were several assassination attempts on world leaders across Europe. Anarchists killed the rulers of France, Spain, Austria, and Italy. Just in case he was a target, too, McKinley received more protection. But it was not enough (as discussed in chapter 1).

Finally Congress ordered the Secret Service to protect the president full-time. Two agents were always in the White House. Several agents took turns standing guard. Whenever Theodore Roosevelt, the new president, left the White House, Secret Service agents went along. In 1906, Roosevelt went to Panama. That was the first time in American history a president left the country while he was in office. Secret Service agents went there too.

Roosevelt called constant protection "a very small but very necessary thorn in the flesh." Some agents had a hard time keeping up with him, since he was an adventurous outdoorsman. He liked to hunt, hike, and camp outdoors. Secret Service agents stopped protecting him after he left office. This turned out to be a mistake. On October 14, 1912, while he was on a campaign stop, he got shot. He was wounded, but he recovered.

In 1917, during World War I, it seemed possible that America's enemies might try to hurt President Woodrow Wilson. Congress then placed his entire family under protection. Ten agents were assigned to the White House. By 1922, 54 policemen patrolled the White House grounds. That year Congress replaced the metropolitan police who had been doing the patrolling with a new White House Police Force. The president was in charge of the White House Police Force until 1930. Then it became a special division of the Secret Service. Other Secret Service agents continued to guard the president inside the White House, too. Their number had risen to 18 by 1939.

An assassination attempt was made on Franklin D. Roosevelt on February 15, 1933. He had already been elected president, but had not yet been sworn into office. He was at an outdoor rally in Miami, Florida, when suddenly a Communist began shouting slogans and firing a

gun at the president-elect. Roosevelt dodged five bullets, but the assassin killed five other people, including the mayor of Chicago. During World War II, Roosevelt traveled all over the world to meet the leaders of America's allies. Secret Service agents always went along—Roosevelt was a very powerful leader whom the Nazis would have been happy to have out of the way.

Adolf Hitler and the Nazi Party may very well have plotted to assassinate President Franklin Delano Roosevelt during World War II.

Until 1940, Secret Service agents just stood guard around the president. They were on the lookout for people who might try to hurt him. But then they started to approach their job differently. Some agents began to investigate *potential* problems. They read the president's mail, looking for threats. When they found out a political group had formed that complained a lot about the government and seemed dangerous, they watched its members.

On November 1, 1950, two men tried to kill President Harry S. Truman in Puerto Rico, a territory of the United States. Some of its residents hope it will one day become a state. But others, called nationalists, want the United States to grant it independence so it can become a new nation. The terrorists who attacked Truman were Puerto Rican nationalists. They believed that he was standing in the way of Puerto Rican independence. They found out the Trumans were living at the vice president's house (their private quarters at the White House needed repairs). One Puerto Rican nationalist went in front of the house and another around back. Both opened fire on the house, hoping to shoot Truman through a window or a door. Agents picked up their own rifles and shot back. Bullets flew through the air until one terrorist dropped dead on the sidewalk. The other sustained a serious wound. One Secret Service agent died, and two more were hurt. But President Truman escaped injury.

In the aftermath of this attack, Congress extended Secret Service protection once more. From that point on, agents would constantly protect the president and his family as well as the president-elect (a person who has been elected president but not yet sworn into office). The new law also said Secret Service agents would protect the vice president whenever he requested it. In 1962, Congress made the list of people the Secret Service protects even longer. The vice president no longer got a choice as to whether or not he wanted bodyguards. The Secret Service started to protect the vice president, the vice president-elect, and former presidents.

In November 1963, President John F. Kennedy planned to travel to five Texas cities. On November 22, he and his wife, Jackie, arrived by plane in Dallas. A huge crowd turned out to greet them. Mrs. Kennedy was presented with flowers. She and the president chatted with well-wishers.

Then they got into a convertible limousine driven by a Secret Service agent. John Connally, governor of Texas, rode along in their car, too. Other cars followed. Their motorcade was going to drive to a building called the Trade Mart, where they were supposed to attend a luncheon. Newspapers had announced the route the motorcade would take so that people could line the streets and watch them pass.

The vice president, Lyndon Baines Johnson, rode behind the Kennedys. Secret Service agents were in his car. Often Secret Service agents rode on the bumper of the president's car, but this did not happen that day. Four police officers rode motorcycles alongside the president's car. A press car, filled with reporters covering the day's events, followed behind.

The presidential limousine made a slow turn from one street onto another. The president, his wife, and Governor Connally talked and laughed, smiling and waving at the people they passed. Suddenly, witnesses heard three shots ring out. John F. Kennedy slumped over. A bullet had gone right into the back of his head, opening his skull. Connally was hit as well and fell onto the car's floorboards. Mrs. Kennedy started to crawl up onto the trunk of the car. Apparently, she was trying to protect her husband, to put her body between him and the unseen gunman. Secret Service agent Clinton J. Hill jumped out of the car behind and ran up to the limousine. He clambered in, shoving Mrs. Kennedy down. Then he shielded her body with his own. By this time, the Secret Service agent driving the car had radioed for instructions on how to get to the nearest hospital.

At 12:34 P.M., reporter Merriman Smith picked up the phone in the press car and called his office. He shouted into the phone, "Three shots were fired at the motorcade!" Instantly, the news was out to newspapers and radio and television stations everywhere.

A Secret Service agent climbs into the back seat of President John F. Kennedy's limousine following the shooting on November 22, 1963, in Dallas, Texas. Many members of the Secret Service openly questioned how well they had done their job that day.

Within minutes the president's car was parked at the hospital's emergency room entrance. Hospital personnel rushed to carry Kennedy and Connally in. Mrs. Kennedy followed. All that was left in the car was the bouquet of roses she'd been given earlier at the airport. Inside an operating room, doctors tried to revive the president, who had stopped breathing. Seeing that a tube inserted in Kennedy's mouth did not help him breathe, Dr. Malcolm Perry cut a hole in his throat and inserted another tube. Again, nothing happened. Kennedy continued to have no heartbeat. Dr. Perry kneaded his chest again and again. Minutes ticked by. He could not bring the president back to life. A priest gave Kennedy the last rites. Mrs. Kennedy stooped to kiss her husband. When the priest said, "Eternal rest, grant him, O Lord," she quietly replied "And let perpetual light shine on him." Then she slipped one of her rings on his finger.

Kennedy was officially declared dead at 1 P.M. A television news crew set up in the hospital. One of the president's staff went on the air to inform the nation the president had died. Lyndon Baines Johnson and his wife, Lady Bird, had been sitting in a waiting room at the hospital. An air force colonel entered the room, carrying a case that always accompanied the president. It contained the codes needed for launching a nuclear attack. Johnson assumed it had been brought there for safekeeping until Kennedy recovered. But then a presidential aide came in. His first words to Johnson were "Mr. President . . ." Johnson looked up, shocked. Lady Bird gasped.

Within minutes the Johnsons were on their way to the Dallas Airport. Soon Secret Service agents brought Mrs. Kennedy and the coffin carrying Kennedy's body as well. A district judge had rushed to join them. They all boarded *Air Force One*, the president's plane. At 2:38 P.M., the judge swore Lyndon Baines Johnson in as the 36th president of the United States.

Within minutes of the shooting, Secret Service agents and policemen had started to investigate. They spread out all over the area where the assassination had taken place. Some went through the Texas School Book Depository, a nearby building where the state kept school textbooks. In an upstairs room, under an open window that looked out on the motorcade route, they discovered discarded fried chicken bones and bullet casings. Obviously a sniper had been there, eating his lunch and waiting for his chance to kill the president.

The depository's staff was able to help them identify a suspect, an employee by the name of Lee Harvey Oswald. A description was circulated, and Oswald was picked up, but only after he had killed a cop. Dragged off to jail, he

Lee Harvey Oswald is seen here being questioned by the media while surrounded by law enforcement officials. Oswald claimed to have been innocent of the shooting, but he was killed by Jack Ruby before he could be tried.

was questioned by police. When they gathered enough evidence, he was charged with the murder. During questioning Oswald never clearly explained why he killed Kennedy. He would never get another chance to explain. The next day, being transferred from the city to a county jail, he was shot to death at point-blank range by a man named Jack Ruby.

To this day, there is controversy about what really happened. Many people believe that the Kennedy assassination was not the act of one man, but part of a conspiracy. Some people think the motorcade was fired on by more than one person. Others think Oswald acted alone but that he had been paid by powerful people to kill Kennedy. Some question whether the Secret Service could have prevented the assassination. Later, agents on duty that day admitted they felt they had failed to do their job. They regretted not insisting that more agents ride in the limousine and not making the president ride in a closed car.

In the years that followed, the Secret Service would work constantly to improve the measures they used to protect the president. Over the years presidents have varied in terms of their relationships with and attitude toward their Secret Service detail. In general, they have been genuinely grateful for the protection they offer. Many have formed friendships with the agents assigned to them, but some have felt a loss of privacy. For close to 90 years, the Secret Service imposed a code of silence on its agents. It prohibited them from ever discussing their work outside of the job. They could never tell reporters, for example, what they knew about a president's private life.

This would change, however, when President Bill Clinton was investigated by a special prosecutor in 1998. Kenneth Starr subpoenaed Secret Service agents to find out what they knew about his relationship with Monica Lewinsky, a former White House intern. The agents protested at being asked to reveal the president's secrets but were ultimately forced to do so.

Today, wherever the president goes, no matter what he does, a group of Secret Service agents guard him. At the White House, there's always a Secret Service agent posted right outside the door of the Oval Office. Should the president leave the White House for a meeting, the Secret Service reviews his plans to make sure they involve as little risk as possible. Agents tag along wherever he goes. When he takes time off to exercise, Secret Service agents go, too. When he was in office, Bill Clinton jogged right in the middle of a crowd of bodyguards. And the Secret Service goes with the president on official trips overseas as well as vacations. Agents don't get much time to sightsee, though. All their time is occupied

Secret Service agents stay on alert during a presidential motorcade. As the role of the Secret Service has increased, so has the number of agents assigned to the president.

with checking and double-checking the president's arrangements and watching out for terrorists.

The Secret Service will never reveal to the public all the measures it takes to protect the president and others. What it will say is that when the president is at home or at work in the White House, it coordinates efforts on the part of the Secret Service Uniformed Division, the Washington, D.C., Metropolitan Police Department, and the

U.S. Park Police to patrol the White House grounds and areas nearby. It also has a Technical Security Division. Before the president travels, agents travel ahead of him to check on the security measures state and local law enforcement officials have made in the various places he'll visit.

The Secret Service agents assigned to protect the president and others have special equipment. They all wear earpieces through which they can receive messages from other agents and the Secret Service command center. Inside their jacket sleeve, they attach a tiny microphone they use to send messages. They wear plain clothes, as opposed to uniforms. This helps them blend into a crowd.

Uniformed agents help keep public places like the White House safe and secure. Countersnipers are

President Bill Clinton jogs with Secret Service agents along the banks of the Moskva River in Moscow. The president is always accompanied by the Secret Service.

The Secret Service uses special K-9 units trained in bomb detection to ensure the president's safety during public appearances.

constantly posted on the roof. Special K-9 teams check cars and deliveries that arrive at the White House. Handlers use specially trained dogs to check for drugs, bombs, and firearms. These dogs are all Belgian Malinois, a breed known for its smarts and its drive to work hard. Each dog lives with his handler, to help create a special bond.

Other uniformed officers are posted around the White House, as well as in front of embassies and the vice president's residence. Every person—whether a tourist, politician, or member of the president's staff—has to go through metal detectors to enter the White House. Officers scan the viewers looking for weapons. A bike patrol rides around the grounds.

In the year 2000, the Secret Service protected the president, vice president, president-elect, and their immediate families; former presidents, their spouses, and any of their children who are under age 16; major presidential and vice presidential candidates; and, in the last four months of an election, candidates' spouses. In 1997, Congress passed a

A Secret Service agent stands at attention during George W. Bush's presidential campaign in 2000. It is one of the many responsibilities of the Secret Service to protect candidates running for major offices in the United States.

new law stating that presidents elected after that date would receive protection for just 10 years after leaving office. This means President Clinton will be the last president to receive lifetime protection.

CHAPTER 4

Money Matters

ONE NOVEMBER DAY IN 1996, five members of the Taftsiou family got into their station wagon in Brooklyn, New York, and headed down the freeway. They drove to a casino in Atlantic City, where they planned to spend a few hours gambling. At first glance, there was nothing unusual about these people. They looked ordinary. They were not high rollers who bet thousands of dollars at a craps table. No, they were just putting a few bills in slot machines.

Suddenly, however, they became the center of attention. Secret Service agents had quietly surrounded them. All five members of the family—Bardul Taftsiou, his 80 year old mother, his wife, and their grown son and daughter—were slapped in handcuffs and hauled off to jail. For five months the Secret Service had been on their trail. For a long time they had suspected these seemingly ordinary people were really big-time counterfeiters. But it took a long time to prove it.

Back at the Taftsiou house, the Secret Service seized a computer and a high-quality color printer. They became evidence at the Taftsious' trial. Bardul and James Taftsiou were accused of having used them to make $1.2 million in counterfeit money. In the comfort of their own living room, they had made piles and piles of fake bills. Some of it they had given to other gamblers to get into circulation. The rest of it they got rid of themselves. They did this by going to Atlantic City and putting bills they had made in a casino's slot machine. When they won, the machine gave them tokens, which they then took to the casino's front desk and turned into real money.

The Taftsious were not the only people running a scam like this. Three years earlier, in 1993, Treasury Department officials admitted that color photocopiers and laser printers were causing them huge problems. Recently both types of machines had gone down in price. This meant many more of them got sold. Most got bought by honest businesses. But counterfeiters purchased them, too.

Computer experts had informed the Treasury Department that they should only expect the problem to get worse. As computers got more accurate, they could be used to make better and better fake money. In 1990, counterfeiters had made $1 million worth of counterfeit money using high-end copiers and printers. Two years later, the total had jumped as high as $8 million. By 2000, a study showed in the '90s, the total might be $2 *billion*.

These facts made the Treasury Department decide to change the design of the $100, $50, and $20 bills. The new bills are designed to be much harder to duplicate. But still, the government warns, Americans should be on the lookout for counterfeits. The Secret Service agency launched a campaign to teach the public how to recognize the real thing.

Of course, the government removes any counterfeit bills it finds from circulation. Consumers and merchants catch some. Banks have special machines now that identify counterfeits. The Federal Reserve has what it calls superscanners. The government will not reveal exactly how they work. But what it will say is that a single machine can inspect 80,000 bills an hour. The machine has 30 different sensors that check everything from the type of paper and ink used to whether the margins are just the right size. After a pile of suspicious bills is made by the machine, a human goes through them, one by one.

The Secret Service has a whole group of agents whose job it is to catch the people who make fakes. In the old days, they could look for people who bought a special kind of paper or lots of black and green ink. Today their job is tougher. The Secret Service says it isn't experts they're looking for anymore but ordinary citizens.

Protecting the president and stopping counterfeiting are the Secret Service's main jobs. Yet the service protects the American public's money in other ways, too. Today, many "identity theft" cases come their way.

One typical identity theft involved a woman named Jessica Grant. One day she went to her bank to take out a loan. She expected the bank to approve the loan at once. After all, she had money saved. And she always paid her bills on time.

But Jessica Grant was in for a terrible shock. Her banker told her he could not loan her any money. The bank had checked with a credit agency. Its records showed she already owed $60,000 to many different companies. She knew that was not true. But it took a long time for her to prove it. Secret Service agents helped her find out that another woman had found out her full name and Social Security number. Using this information, she had taken out loans in Jessica Grant's name to buy two cars and a trailer. The woman had also gotten credit cards using Jessica's name and gone on many shopping sprees.

The Secret Service says it believes that identity fraud cost its victims $745 million in 1997. By now the total is even more. Agents investigate hundreds of thousands of cases of identity fraud a year.

They also try to stop credit card crime. In the 1980s, banks and consumer groups began to issue many warnings. Thieves were stealing not just credit cards but the carbon paper that is left after a cashier passes a credit card through a machine to record a purchase. Cashiers put the carbons in the trash, not realizing a thief can read credit card numbers on them. Criminals also stole mail, looking for people's bank statements or bills that might show a credit card number. Some criminals made a career of stealing credit card numbers and using them. Rings of credit card thieves developed.

In 1984, after Congress made fraudulent use of credit cards a violation of federal law (rather than a state crime), the Secret Service assumed responsibility for investigating such fraud. When ATMs (automatic teller machines) sprouted up, thieves began to steal those receipts, too, to get people's account information. The Secret Service also stepped in to try to prevent those crimes.

When computer use became widespread, Congress asked the agency to investigate computer fraud whenever there was a federal interest. This means that Secret Service agents try to prevent the tampering of computers carrying government records. They also investigate when a computer crime involves the government.

In recent years, "hackers" have made a lot of headlines. They are criminals who steal or figure out computer passwords. From their own computers, they access a computer somewhere else. Sometimes they just look at a file and record what is there. Other times they alter files. Either way, they can do tremendous damage. This includes when money is illegally transferred, for example, or government documents or records are stolen using an Internet connection.

Early in 2000, a Canadian teenager using the name "Mafiaboy" shut down huge companies' websites for

A man wishing to be known only as "Mudge" describes to a Senate subcommittee the relative ease of "hacking." During his testimony, Mudge claimed that security on the Internet is so lax that hackers could entirely disable it within a half hour.

several hours two days in a row. He caused the sites to lose a large amount of business, totaling millions of dollars. This case made newspaper headlines around the world. Cases the Secret Service investigates often do *not* make the news. The government does not want to let people know what kind of information can be or has been stolen. After all, its computer files include a lot of classified information, such as exactly what kind of weapons the military owns.

Following holiday services, President Clinton and his family share a laugh as they leave church. But in the background, an ever watchful Secret Service agent remains close at hand.

CHAPTER **5**

The Future

TODAY, SECRET SERVICE AGENTS have an extremely important responsibility: protecting both the nation's leaders and its money. In the future, the Secret Service's job is sure to become more complex.

After World War II ended, the two most powerful nations on earth, the United States and the Soviet Union, became enemies. During the Cold War, each side stood ready to go to war at a moment's notice. Both nations built a vast number of nuclear weapons. Many times it seemed possible that one side would launch its missiles. Had this happened, some of the biggest cities in the world might have been wiped out within minutes.

It was an incredibly dangerous time. The world rejoiced when the Soviet Union collapsed, and the Cold War ended. In the 1960s and 1970s, the Secret Service had considered Soviet spies the biggest threat to the president. Agents assigned to protect him spent a great deal of their time investigating Soviets who came to the United States, trying to find out exactly what they meant to do here.

Today the once-vast Soviet Union has been broken into many smaller countries. In some ways, this has created big new problems for the people charged with protecting the president. There is a more unpredictable world order. Superpowers are no longer on the brink of war. But smaller wars have recently broken out all over the world. Different ethnic and religious groups fight for control of many countries. Many of these fights include groups that do not hesitate to use terrorism as a way to win. In Libya, for example, extremists have plotted to kill world leaders in order to demonstrate their country's strength.

Secret Service agents believe many more threats exist now than in the past. Trying to identify who might pose a threat is a big challenge. Investigators spend a great deal of time going over reports that American diplomats and spies send home from other countries. They are trying to find out exactly which foreigners may be plotting to kill the president and other American leaders. Agents also keep track of groups of Americans who express unhappiness with the government. They realize that these people, too, may be willing to kill or die in the hope of bringing about radical change.

Another problem the Secret Service faces is that new weapons are constantly being invented. Many of the newest are very small and easy to hide. Some very powerful guns are small enough to fit in the palm of your hand. Many assassins also use disguised weapons. In 1978, a Bulgarian leader was killed when a Soviet spy holding an umbrella bumped up against him. What the Bulgarian did not realize was that the umbrella had been equipped with a tiny pin that sent poison into his bloodstream.

As the job required of the Secret Service becomes increasingly difficult, new tools are deployed to increase its effectiveness. Advances in technology, such as this satellite being placed in orbit, allow the Secret Service to keep an even closer eye on the safety of the president.

The Secret Service agents who protect the nation's money also face new challenges. Criminals are very inventive. They continually think of new ways to use computers to steal money or information. There are also hackers who simply want to cause trouble.

Officials do not like to tell the public much about computer hacking into government computers. But what we do know is that a large number of Secret Service agents are assigned to computer crime cases. Others investigate other types of crime that involve high-tech equipment. Even though the Treasury Department has just issued newly designed money, Secret Service agents stay on the lookout for counterfeiters.

New technology does create many problems for the Secret Service. But at the same time, it also gives Secret Service agents better tools with which to fight criminals.

The computers they use to investigate crimes are extremely powerful. They have access to satellite systems that can provide photos of any place in the world at a moment's notice. The agents that protect the president and other leaders often get new and improved weapons and equipment as well.

Recently, the Secret Service showed it was thinking very seriously about the future. In January 2000, the agency started to run advertisements in newspapers. The agency was in the process of creating hundreds of new jobs and needed to hire people to fill them. It especially wanted computer experts and engineers.

The Secret Service has an extremely important job. In the future, it promises to become harder. But the agency is already preparing for the tasks ahead. It does excellent jobs now of protecting both the nation's leaders and its money, which are some of the most important jobs of all.

Glossary

Agency—An office that is part of a bigger department in the U.S. government.

Anarchist—Someone who believes that all governments should be brought down so people can rule themselves.

Assassin—Someone who kills a leader.

Assassination—Murder, especially of a political leader.

Counterfeiting—The copying or forging of money or other documents.

Depression—A period during which the economy slows down drastically and people lose a lot of money.

Engraving—A printing process for pictures in which an image is carved into a metal plate. When the lines carved into the plate are filled with ink, it is pressed onto paper to print the picture.

Fraud—Cheating.

Immigrants—People who come to one country from another to live.

Investigating—Using the detective process of law enforcement officials to solve crimes.

Landslide—A huge majority of votes.

Tenements—Large, poorly built apartment buildings.

Terrorist—Someone who uses violence to change a society or government.

Further Reading

Ameringer, Charles D. *U.S. Foreign Intelligence: The Secret Side of American History.* Lexington, Massachusetts: Lexington Books, 1990.

Andrew, Christopher. *For the President's Eyes Only.* New York: Harper-Collins, 1995.

Jeffrey-Jones, Rhodri. *American Espionage: From Secret Service to the CIA.* New York: The Free Press, 1977.

Johnson, David R. *Illegal Tender: Counterfeiting and the Secret Service in Nineteenth Century America.* Washington: Smithsonian Institution Press, 1995.

Miller, Nathan. *Spying for America: The Hidden History of U.S. Intelligence.* New York: Paragon House, 1989.

United States Secret Service Home Page—http://www.treas.gov/usss/

Wilkie, Don. *American Secret Service Agent.* New York: Frederick A. Stokes, 1934.

Index

Adams, John Quincy, 30-31
Air Force One, 43
American Revolution, 17-18
Anarchists, 11
Art of War, The, 17
Assassination, 24-25, 58
  attempts, 29-30, 31-32,
    38-39, 40
  presidential, 11-13, 34-35,
    36, 37, 41-44
  threat of, 14, 18, 37
ATMs (automatic teller
  machines), 54

Booth, John Wilkes, 34-36
Brady, James, 30

Civil War, 18-19, 20, 32,
  33, 34
Cleveland, Grover, 37
Clinton, Bill, 45, 49
Cold War, 57-58
Computer fraud, 54, 59
Congress, 13, 19, 23, 32, 35,
  37, 38, 54
  extension of Secret Service
    protection by, 40
  new limits on Secret Service
    protection set by, 48-49
  orders presidential protection,
    37-38
Connally, John, 41, 42
Counterfeiting, 13, 19, 21-23,
  51-53, 59
Credit card crime, 54
Crockett, Davy, 32
Czolgosz, Leon, 11, 12, 13

Department of Justice, 27

Federal Bureau of Investigation
  (FBI), 27
Ford's Theater, 33, 34

Garfield, James, 36
Grant, Jessica, 53
Grant, Ulysses S., 33
Guiteau, Charles J., 36

Hackers, 13, 54-55, 59
Hale, Nathan, 18
Harris, Clara, 33
Hill, Clinton J., 41

Identity fraud/theft, 13-14,
  53-54
Illegal immigration, 25-26
Illegal voting, 24
Internet, 54-55

Jackson, Andrew, 31-32
Jefferson, Thomas, 30
Johnson, Lady Bird, 43
Johnson, Lyndon Baines, 41, 43
Johnston, Joseph, 33

Kennedy, Jackie, 40-44
Kennedy, John F., 40-43

Land fraud, 24
Lawrence, Richard, 31-32
Lee, Robert E., 33
Lewinsky, Monica, 45
Lincoln, Abraham, 18-19, 32-36
Lincoln, Mary, 33, 35

Madison, James, 30
Mafiaboy, 54-55
Mail robbery, 24
McKinley, William, 9, 10-13,
  37

Oswald, Lee Harvey, 43-44
Oval Office, 45

Pan-American Exposition,
  10-11
Parker, John F., 33-34
Perry, Malcolm, 42
Pinkerton, Allan, 18-19

Rathbone, Henry, 33, 35
Reagan, Ronald, 29-30
Roosevelt, Franklin Delano,
  38-39
Roosevelt, Theodore, 11-13, 38
Ruby, Jack, 44

Secret Service Uniformed
  Division, 46
Sherman, William, 33
Spanish-American War, 9,
  26, 37
Spies, 17-19, 20, 23, 26,
  57-58
Starr, Kenneth, 45

Taftsiou, Bardul, 51-52
Taftsiou, James, 52
Technical Security Division,
  47
Terrorists, 13, 15, 58
Texas School Book Depository,
  43
Treasury Department, 19, 21,
  23, 27, 52, 59
Truman, Harry S., 40
Tyler, John, 32

U.S. Park Police, 47
U.S. Secret Service, 44
  agents, 10, 13-14, 20, 21,
    22-23, 24-27, 29
  duties of, 13-15, 24-25,
    53-54
  establishment of, 18-19
  presidential protection, 13,
    30, 37, 38, 39, 45-49,
    57-58

Walker, Joseph A., 24-25
War of 1812, 30
Washington, George, 17,
  18, 30
Washington, Martha, 30
White House, 9, 29, 30, 32, 36,
  37, 38, 40, 45, 46
  security, 47-48
White House Police Force,
  38
Whitley, Hiram C., 21
Wilkie, Don, 22, 25-26
Wilson, Woodrow, 38
Wood, William P., 19-20
World War I, 38
World War II, 39, 57

ABOUT THE AUTHOR: Ann Graham Gaines is a freelance author who specializes in writing nonfiction for children. She has written a dozen books. She has master's degrees in library science and American studies from the University of Texas at Austin. She lives in the woods near Gonzales, Texas, with her four children, all readers.

SENIOR CONSULTING EDITOR Arthur M. Schlesinger, jr. is the leading American historian of our time. He won the Pulitzer Prize for his book *The Age of Jackson* (1945) and again for *A Thousand Days* (1965). This chronicle of the Kennedy Administration also won a National Book Award. Professor Schlesinger is the Albert Schweitzer Professor of the Humanities at the City University of New York, and he has been involved in several other Chelsea House projects, including the REVOLUTIONARY WAR LEADERS and COLONIAL LEADERS series.